CONSTELLATION

A poetry collection

LINA KATSORCHI

CONSTELLATION – A poetry collection by Lina Katsorchi

Published by Lina Katsorchi (Independent publication)

ISBN: 978-1-912315-81-9 (Paperback, Ingram)
ISBN: 978-1-91231582-6 (Paperback, Amazon)
ISBN: 978-191231583-3 (Ebook, Epub)
ASIN: B083ZGPJ14 (Ebook, Kindle/Amazon)

Imprint: Stergiou Books Limited
Distribution and publishing rights (for distribution use and market availability only): Worldwide, non-exclusive (Stergiou Book Limited)
Main distributors: Stergiou Books Limited, Ingram, Amazon)
Design: Stergiou Books Limited
Front cover: Canva/Pixabay

Available copies from the libraries: Irish Copyright Agency, The National Library of Ireland, The British Library, National Library of Scotland, National Library of Wales, Cambridge University, Oxford University (Bodleian Library), Trinity College, NUI (Cork, Galway, Maynooth), University College (Belfield), University of Limerick, Dublin City University.

stergioubooks.com

To Christina, who is music to the lines of my life

"Thou, who hast given me eyes to see
and love this sight so fair,
give me a heart to find out thee,
and read thee everywhere."

— *John Keeble*

Contents

CHAPTER 1

"A love that's poetry turned into song"

I

I want a world where I can hold your hand
without letting it go when prying eyes
observe us, free to live a love unplanned
away from all the cold society's spies.
I want a world arrested when our lips
are locked, a heartbeat's sweet surrender to
that moment when my fingers touch your hips
and silence whispers how I long for you.

II

What is that word, always? What does it mean?
is it a slice of time that will elude
us when we reach for it, a place we've been
but never knew, the smile that we once viewed?
That word, always— so many meanings, yet
just one is ours. So press your chest to mine
and listen to our whispering hearts that met
to race together; that one beat, that line
that sings between our sighs with a bass voice
is "always"; it is our love, it is our choice.

III

Anywhere we go
our love is the luggage
we take with us
It is a large suitcase
with the contents of a
treasure box
and the depth of

a magical chest
And on our back
a backpack of our most
beautiful memories
and empty bags
for all our new moments
And thus we go
to the end of the world
and back
packed and in love forever.

IV

As sure as the bee landing on the flower
and feeding on a nectar never tried,
as fierce as sea-waves crushing with the power
of impassioned storms which create the tide—
As soft as quiet gusts of wind that meet
as opposites but madly intertwine
to form tornados, as pure as the sweet
surrender of stars falling when they most shine—
As clouds colliding, roaring thunders, rain
cascading to water the withered ground—
thus, with a yearning that could not restrain
our lips anymore, inside a kiss we drowned.
Flying across a universe of bliss—
the feeling of our first and every kiss.

V

For years I've been a short unfinished poem
with almost rhymes and stained mixed metred lines
full of deleted stanzas since the dream

of life escaped me, false words I erased
and wrote again, although no harmony
combined them so I could not reach the end.
For years you've been a sweet unfinished song
with missing lyrics and mistaken chords,
untuned to what your mind sought, for the truth
of life escaped you, melodies mismatched
with what you wrote, and so you sang
the thoughts of others that came close to yours.
Yet now we found that we two rhyme together,
that I'm the lyrics for the tune you hear,
and you the lines of my final couplet,
a love that's poetry turned into song
which only you can sing and I recite,
in harmony the words and music; whole.

VI

This is the last image I always see
before I close my eyes, lingering behind
them after: Your face is leaning towards me
slowly; your eyes are shut, as though resigned
to the most peaceful sleep, with dreams made of
your heart's favourite roller coasters, such as
sweets and songs and me. It may be your love
for ripe strawberries with sugar that has
parted your lips and purses them forth to
savour the sweetness. A fog blinds my sight
but still I wonder what powder did you
use on your cheeks, is it the light of night
or your heart's favourite, Love? That is mine
too! There are twisted knots about your hair,
I swear they are roses gifted to the shrine

of your beauty. This— then there's nothing there
anymore to see, but feel how with a kiss
our lips bring to life all our dreams of bliss.

VII

My love meets your love in the sky
like dragons tangled in a dance,
brought together by what was chance
but feels to them like destiny.
A single flap of the wings makes
the world shake, and as they respire,
out of their mouths come sighs of fire
that pierce the darkness in their wake.
They bring the dawn, they bring the storm,
and conquer the skies. They will burn
to ashes those who dare to turn
against them. And so they perform;
the amorous dance of dragons, capable
of stirring up the cosmos. Chest
to chest, carrying with them their nest,
together they're invincible.

VIII

My kisses to your hair shall be like sheets
of handwritten poems scattered in the wind,
tangled with leaves as they fly through the streets
carried in tiny tornadoes. One will get pinned
against each window and against each wall
of every city, against each bush and tree
of every living forest, and thus all
will feel through rhymes what it is like to be
in love so deeply it makes your heart shake—

like so, my lips shall touch each curl of long
brown hair and bestow kisses that will wake
you to feelings that are everything but wrong:
A passion that turns a kiss into ecstasy,
a love that's best expressed in poetry.

IX

Dear heart, I will follow you like the moon
orbits the earth — constant— and like a tune
is coupled with the lines in harmony.
Wherever you are, that's where I will be;
for we go together like the true light
comes with the sun, inseparable like the night
from the stars, and the truth from poetry.
So if you look behind these words, you'll see
there's a chain that ties your heart to my heart;
it's called love, and we'll never be apart.

X

Wait for me as the west waits for the sun—
in silence, patiently, and mostly sure,
watching me travel across skies that cannot stun
my destined course. I am coming to moor
in your arms, and then the most beautiful sunset
will become your eyes. I ask, wait for me
like the flower waits for her bee to get
a smell of her sweetness— anxiously, impatiently,
uncertainly, not taking for granted such
a miracle like making honey together, although
I know, and you feel too, I will not touch

another's petals, no nectar will flow
upon my lips but yours only. Love— wait
for me like the atmosphere waits to greet
a falling star— desirous of the fate
of igniting together and certain to meet.

XI

Yes, there are ways to measure love—
We count it with the grains of rice
you push into my plate so that our meals
are made equal and with the times
I've offered you my black leather gloves
although I know you hate them
because I want you to be safe and warm.
We count it with the creaks of the door
each time it opens and we're home
and with the frequent charging of
our phones after those long days apart.
Love is the total of the times I've touched
your hand though you are eating
and the occasions you offered to help
me stand when I was in pain despite
knowing I'm too proud to accept.
Love is calculated with the songs and poems
we send each other when our hearts speak
in a language complex for the mind.
We even count it with our fears and tears
and nightmares because if it wasn't
so precious we wouldn't fear to lose it.
And yes, love is measured in the times
you said we cannot measure love
and every time I proved you wrong.

XII

The world is like a puzzle scattered on
the floor, the pieces all over the place,
some may be damaged and some even gone;
so who is to say if they will embrace
one day as whole? Perhaps it cannot be
anymore, it's been a mess for too long.
And that 'cause some of the pieces are free
in their own will, even connecting wrong
for a while, whereas some others wait to
be put in a place that must be right by
some invisible hands. In this mess, you
and I came together, pieces that tie
perfectly; we have found our correct slot,
so who cares the rest of the world does not.

XIII

There is a poem in my heart
metred by its racing beats
but I have not translated
its meaning as of yet,
for I have not mastered
the language it is in;
but our kisses teach me
its limitless vocabulary,
I always have more to learn;
and our caresses teach me
its unique grammatical rules,
the basic one being
our fingers intertwined;
and as we're making love
the syntax is created,

infinite number of sentences
to calculate our passion;
our smiles, our laughs,
our tears and loving words
the punctuation of our love
and our goodbyes a comma
in a language with no full stop.

CHAPTER 2

"Safe in the shelter of our love's embrace"

I

On a winter night, sheltered in a car
at the top of a mountain where no star
could see us, no wind move us, we were kissed
by the storm, and suddenly all we missed
till then was gone. Thundering passion in
the skies of the heart, across the skin
lightings of yearning, and with a kiss the break
of the tempest. Caresses that could shake
the clouds and part the heavens were our guide
to undiscovered heights. We flew outside
the limits, where looking at you meant to recognise
my future. This is how I found in your eyes
our parallel universe, the world we brought
to life after creating it with wanton thought,
and never shall we fall now from Love's height,
for it has become our ground since that night.

II

Last night we found out that we are chess queens
following a course that's bound to make us collide
in a game where there is no winner or loser,
but as our paths meet, we both win a victory
in love, and slide away from the board where
pawns pretend to threaten us, thinking we can't
elude their leisure motions. Such is the power
of love and the world its domain, where we
as sovereigns can even uncross the constellations
and cross them anew. We discovered The Big Frying Pan,
listened to the music of the shadows, but I ask you
now, what is the constellation formed between us?

What is the melody we hear each time our hands touch?
Our side by side royal steps and our affectionate looks
illuminate the darkness, for we teach this world how
the beauty of love lives in the majesty of simplicity.

III

Twin flames are burning at the table's side,
waltzing around to the changes in the air,
concurrent steps as though their aligned stride
was being rehearsed for centuries. A pair
of candles, lit and wasting simultaneously,
bring signs of dawn to the darkness and write
with the ink of shadows their own poetry
on the walls. In their lines lives a night
when you were dressed in firelight and you laid
your body in my arms, hiding your heart
into my chest. In passion's fumes we made
love endlessly; climax was just another start
of the blaze that binds us, a strange harmony
that like the flames in sync moved us about.
What is the difference between us? Easy—
we, unlike the flames, will never burn out.

IV

Can you feel that it was love at first touch
of our lips? They collided with so much
passion that the world disappeared inside
the fumes of a kiss, a storm that cannot subside.
A touch that pierced so deeply into my soul,
it soothed my heart and filled with dreams the hole

I bore, and even my bones seemed to forget
all my life's grief, and smiled as our lips met.
A touch that cannot ever know an end,
for one night sealed a love that can transcend
place and time. Our tongues are moving like the sea,
lips locked in a kiss that lasts for eternity.

V

Outside our fears were falling in the rain
but disappeared once they have hit the ground,
our pains flared the sky with each lighting's vein
but faded once they heard the thunder's sound.
We sat cheek to cheek, watching their demise,
safe in the shelter of our love's embrace,
no more touched by them. I saw in your eyes
a rainbow waiting to arise, and in your face
the clearing of the gloomy clouds; the scent
of the soaked grass held the wish for tranquillity
but as the rain stopped, my kiss on your forehead meant
it is more than a wish, but a reality
to come, and it is ours. As hand in hand we go,
I promise you our whole life will be so.

VI

The radio dissolved into the evening air
and gave rhythm to the dance of the rain,
and the notes got tangled up in your hair
so I reached to touch them. In the refrain
of a slow lovesong, that is where we found
each other; in an embrace that felt like melody

to our yearning bodies. Our words were drowned
by the tune of growing love. What bond could be
more magical than the one that is song,
sung from my harp-like touch upon your breast
or the way you roll your hips with mine along?
We heard it first, then it was all expressed,
a hum that became deafening with desire's might,
and we've been united in music since that night.

VII

The clocks struck twelve and above us the sky
ignited with fireworks as though our heart
was being reflected in the stars. A sigh
came from the crowd with wishes for the start
of the new year. Voices cheering around
us, sea-waves, sand and pebbles clapping for
the dancing of bonfires to the musical sound
of shooting flares, and the promise of more
blissful moments was in the wind. And yet
nothing had really changed. Maybe the rest
need an excuse for joy, not we— lips met,
fingers intertwined, thunders in our breast
made us tremble with joy, like yesterday,
last month, today and tomorrow. Upon the shore
of our city, drunk and embraced we laughed away
the years, happy and more loved than ever before.

VIII

We were at the top of a funfair wheel
but felt like being at the top of the world;
above the sky itself, with my arm curled

around you, what's thought magic was then real.
And if you'd listen close, you'd realise
the rest of the fair had faded away
as we flew on between the flickering play
of crimson lights, which gave your chestnut eyes
a touch of green and amber; was it true?
I think we floated on a cloud indeed
when lost in an unending kiss our locked lips led
us even higher. A roof of stars, a view
of a world made for us, our breath the only sound,
a hope that we may never reach the ground.

CHAPTER 3

"To kill her pain, I turned my love to medicine"

I

Dear heart, if I had the power to create
anything, then the first thing I would make
is a series of dreams, so every night
with a kiss on your head I could excite
their vision in your fancy. Then, behind
closed eyelids you would find futures designed
and in them all we'd be together. No
more nightmares, just peace. You know,
sometimes sleep reminds me a lot of the sea;
you can see the furious waves or you can see
the beautiful coral reefs below.
Therefore these dreams would be equipment so
you can breathe despite the waves and behold
the seashells in your mind of blue and gold.
Words, light your fires, we have work to do!
Create dreams! O love, I'd do anything for you!

II

Your tears wrote on the sheet like they were ink
on paper, black, full of a sadness old
but constantly renewed, like quills must sink
in bottles to refill — the tale you told
was the most beautiful tragedy I've read,
but I could not help but feel the despair
of wanting to change the ending that led
to this girl who lacks but deserves more care
than a plain heart can give — inside these eyes
are hidden stories of a past that stands
like the last draft, a script you can't revise,
but can read differently when in my hands
your face is nestled safe, and on your cheek
my lips taste your tears with the love you seek.

III

Your battered angry heart, show it to me,
unfold new awful flaws before my eyes
and wait for me to turn away and flee
in terror; wait, and you will realise
the more I know you, the more I love you.
What ever was that was merely benign?
Shadows lurk under the moonlight, the sea's blue
hides reefs of shipwrecks, a rose's design
includes bloomed thorns and petals, and none of
these hold a place in my heart like you do.
Do you think I'm a fool mistaking love
for idealisation? Would you rethink if you knew
I count your flaws before I sleep at night
as though they are the brightest stars I've seen?
A lifetime runs on both darkness and light,
beside you spent, my love, never again alone.

IV

I have been thinking baby birds don't need
to grow too much in order to take wing—
all they need is true love. And so they'll feed
from a mouth that cares for them, they will cling
to that embrace that feels the warmest. Day
by day they will be given fondness in
their nest and when they choose to go away
it won't be 'cause they're strong enough to win
all battles but because the safety
and affection gave them the courage to defy
their fears. So one day they jump from the tree
only to realise that they can fly.

V

You told me demons haunt you since you were
a child, and sometimes I have seen them too,
their cruel shadow following you anywhere
but in my arms; you told me that you drew
safe walls around you, scared to face the world
that showed you all its naked cruelty.
Thus you came to me, in the darkness curled
and broken, and as I pulled you to me
I swore you won't need walls again but these,
which are not cold and frigid, but with care
locked tight around you, eager to appease
the fiends in you, and strong enough to bear
your heaviest burdens. This is your nest; stay,
I'll keep you safe, and drive the wraiths away.

VI

Beloved, for you I will make a bandage of
the sun and wrap all of your wounds of darkness,
till they stop bleeding and you are fearless
before them, holding onto the power of love.
Room by room, the prison inside your mind
will collapse and its black walls will melt down,
touched by the warm sunlight that will surround
you— one day nothing will be left behind
but stone discolouring under the sun. Then you
and I will look at your scars and laugh through
the night, 'cause like a child that runs around
with excitement, you once fell on flat ground.

VII

I held a sad girl in my arms tonight
and I loved her despite the tears that rolled
onto my breast - as the stars in the night
of her eyes fell for me, I swore I'd hold
the skies on my shoulders for her alone -
and had she known each of her tears for me
was but a wish for sunrise - had she known
she is my brightest day of all, could she
still love me? could I show her she's the sun—
though dark sometimes, my dawn, my only one.

VIII

I wish I could transform my arms to wings
that would protect this small caged bird that sings
of freedom; you. Hide in my feathers, fly
away with me, to the peak of the sky
and back down to a hollow in a tree
where we can build a nest for you and me,
our future family. I will show you
a world where hungry vultures don't pursue
your anxious flight, where heights do not breed fear
into your heart, and I sing "I am here
for you" each morning with the earliest lark.
And when you sleep, I'll stand guard in the dark
until your wings are strong to flutter on their own.
The memory of the cage and of being alone
will fade, you'll find your singing voice anew,
and fly to freedom with me always next to you.

IX

I woke and found your heart wrapped in my arm,
the brightest diamond shattered from the harm
it has endured, yet with the beauty of sunrise,
promising peace as you do with your eyes.
She coughed then and I thought she had a cold,
but she said no; for years she tried to hold
the sick on her shoulders that she too caught
an illness that keeps creeping in her thought.
Her fever was light, so to kill her pain
I turned my love to medicine, gave care to chain
the virus; I took the shatters and I kissed
them till they could be glued together and exist
as whole again. Your diamond heart gave signs
of light; I'll be here to make sure she shines.

X

My love will be
the mending of your bleeding skin —
for I will kiss your wounds
till flowers grow out of them
and I will turn your scars
into the most crimson of roses
painted by the bloody tears
of your kind weeping heart —
I will cut and place them on the grave
of your one day deceased sorrows
until the stone is covered fully
by roots and withered leaves
and the tomb disappears
lost in the forest of your strengths —

No memorial for these griefs!
the dead will be sometimes remembered
yet they won't be around you
anymore.

XI

Sadly there will come days when you will feel
two invisible hands pushing you down.
You'll fall, maybe bleed, and carry a frown
on your forehead awhile. And then your meal
will be a bit more cooked than it should be
and less tasty because, damn, you forgot
the salt. In that moment some frantic thought
will poison your mind and you will not see
the shower water is no doubt the right
temperature. And then you will walk cold
back into the room, drop your shirt, and scold
yourself you didn't mop the floor last night,
though it was just your fingers were trembling.
Then, darling, when everything seems to be working
against you, find the truth inside my eyes and say
after me: "it is nothing more than a bad day".

XII

Go coldly quiet, tell me to leave you
alone, 'cause you are angry and can't face
yourself, but to me that's a reason to
stay and let you cry in my warm embrace.
Ask me a thousand times if I truly
love you, if I want us, if I won't go

where you are not one day; all this to me
is reason to stay and make it all so.
Bewitch me with a smile, don't let me seek
you next to me at night, give me a kiss
that sets the world on fire, caress my cheek,
behold me staying to have more of this.
Darling, don't you see everything you do
to me is a reason to stay with you?

XIII

Beloved, take my hand and we'll fly away
to a forest that's still green and our song
still but not for long unsung. A new day
is dawning so why chase the night? So long
we lived in darkness, sleeping, haunted by
the nightmare of bloodthirsty bird of prey.
But now we've woken to the bluest sky,
to a path of sunlight that shows the way
to our new nest, so let me be your wings
and I will raise you so high the world will
look minor. Can you hear how my heart sings
to inspire your song too, hot with the thrill
of soaring into the daylight? There's no height
that can scare us— we are ready to take flight!

CHAPTER 4

"Our shadows danced like moving galaxies"

I

My love, we are not teachers or scholars
nor could we ever be— we were not born
for that, they are just dreams we have
awake. Dearest, you and I are astronomers
brave enough to do what no one else did—
not just study outer space from afar
on endless nights wasted above a glass
of amber alcohol, trying to solve its
mysteries with thought. Darling, we are
astronomers who travelled to the cosmos
and stepped even further than astronauts.
What a revelation was waiting for us there!
A whole new universe dominated our reality,
more real, yet present for a long time,
although our eyes had not adjusted yet to
the light of a different sun. We can't
go back now— light years separate us
from that world. And why go back? My sweet,
will you pilot our course while I sit here
admiring these new nebulas gleaming on
your freshly washed hair and the astral
explosions taking place in your eyes?
Will you stay and range over the corners,
the edges, the chaos, and the forces of
gravity that pull us together? Will you
stay and explore this universe with me?

II

Each time she touches the guitar I swear
that her hands orchestrate the universe.
She combs the strings and melodies disperse

the galaxies across the skies and scare
the void away. I've felt her voice command
the stars to shine for me tonight— they obeyed.
When I close my eyes I hear her songs played
between the planets, as though to expand
the cosmos, though the chords like gravity
are holding it together at the same time.
Her music is my world— and thus I count my time
in song but my love in infinity.

III

You looked up at the night sky and you said
we are nothing compared, a grain of sand
in the endless beach of the cosmos, a shred
of life too small to make a change and stand
before the void — O but how my heart disagrees!
for I see we don't even have to say a word
but our silence brings the collide of galaxies,
our stares meeting creating a new world
with their energy. And as our arms embrace
we glow brighter than all the suns! We disperse
with kisses stars before the reach of space,
for with the power of love we have defied the universe.

IV

The candles were the stars in the nightsky
of our love, and they did not need to fall,
for our kisses were enough to realise
the wishes of our hearts. Against the wall
our shadows danced like moving galaxies,

and the red roses were the planets where
our future lives, sustained by the gravity
of passion. In such moments, dear, I swear
our universe is so vast that no one
else could ever comprehend it. The sound
of soft music was the voice of the sun,
reminding us our days together abound,
measured in countless years of light,
travelling through spacetime as outlined
in our eyes, when we had dinner one night
and made love like two galaxies aligned.

V

On a summer night as we sat by the sea
the whole world was plunged to silence, and we
fell in the embrace of the universe.
I could not tell if the lights that dispersed
around us belonged to the town anymore,
or if the stars had come down to adore
the earth, in a moment passionately entwined.
And we looked up at what transcends the mind,
a cosmos we can never bear to understand
in our humanly confinement. Yet here we stand,
two trivial specks of life before the vast
complexities of space, actresses cast
a cameo role in the one-time staged play
of being. Yet holding you close, I must say
that although we are slaves to volatile chance,
placed and moved in the world akin to the dance
of the sea-waves that could go anywhere,
I feel so lucky I was brought here to share
my minor existence with you. O love, can you

fathom it? Hold my hand, behold the view
of the uncaring, expanding universe above
that could do anything, and led us to this love.

CHAPTER 5

"To my fears, to them promise your never, dear"

I

Your absence is a poem of its own,
but it is not what you will read tonight;
this is no poem but my wet cheekbone
where tears are busy learning how to write.
The night-sky misses no star that must fall
for he has plenty still; but if the dark
itself faded away, he'd lose it all.
Dawn is extolled by the song of each lark,
so when one dies, she still can hear the rest;
but if they all decided not to sing,
she would lose half the beauty she possessed.
Most flowers bloom evergreen at break of spring,
so nobody observes the withered one
that has been cut, for still the others' scent
prevails; but if winter lasted longer than
it should, all blossoming flowers would be spent.
See, you are not one out of many to me,
but you are all, you're everything; you go,
and the world goes with you. I cannot be,
I am not me, with you is the me that I know.
Your absence is a poem of its own
but it is not what you have read tonight;
this is no poem but my wet cheekbone
where tears express what words just can't say right.

II

I was holding you when I woke up, though
your smell did not caress me to reality.
Sleepily my fingers then tried to flow
through your locks, but I found none would be

twisted around their edges. I sought to hide
my face in your cleavage, to refuge in
your loving embrace, at home by your side,
but I could not feel the warmth of your skin.
I called your name but you were sleeping
still, I thought, why else would you not call mine
in response? No doubt you were wandering
in some dream I could wake you from and combine
our breaths into mutual whispers of
adoration— I love you. But to open my eyes
hurt me this morning. Where were you, my love?
My heart will ache if I don't memorise
the taste of your lips even for a day.

III

How long until those monsters in
my head are unleashed in the world? Until
the battle becomes real, until your will
is broken, your sword rusty and they win?
How long before one of the reasons to
leave me becomes strong enough, you cannot
defeat it anymore, before this thought
becomes a tyrant, commanding what to do?
The fear— sometimes it comes to me at night
like visions of a madman that won't go away,
and follows like a sleeping shadow in the day,
an ethereal presence with a venomous bite.
Each minute is a possibility drawing near,
but I love and I burn!— so I beg you—
to my heart, promise your future, but to
my fears, to them promise your never, dear.

IV

I have no idea what to write tonight,
as nothing seems willing to speak to me;
perhaps the stars are not positioned right
when you're not here, and the winds disagree.
Sorrow knows no language but that of tears
and I've been fluent all my life until
I loved you; but when your face disappears
sometimes, I fear I will again fall ill
with grief. Don't be my moon, for the moon hides
partly and then completely, leaving me alone
in the dark. Don't be my sun, for the sun slides
into the west and takes too long till dawn.
Be my blue sky and never hide, never leave—
but I cannot see you now, only lament
the ceiling keeping me from trying to believe
and not just hope. Tonight the crickets torment
my thought and I do not know what to do
but write about the painful wait for you.

V

Beloved, when you're gone away
your scent remains with me
like the fragment of a dream
that's drifting through
my memory — incomplete
and though i catch myself
striving throughout the day
to capture glimpses and recall
of the dream in its entirety
what use is trying to remember

when sooner or later
you will return and I will live
within the dream of you
which is complete and real?

VI

Far from the reach of my protective wing,
you fly on your own, battered and afraid,
while I sit here upon a tree and sing
of your return to the safe nest we made.
Far from the field of my safeguarding view,
you wander in the dark without a chart,
while I glow brightly, a lighthouse for you
till you sail back to the warmth of my heart.
Far from my touch, far from my sight, but in
my thoughts forever; next to me
in imaginings way stronger than reality,
this is how my love dreams. Dear one, hear me;
Nothing can divide us, not even time or space,
for we are joined weightless, endless in an embrace.

CHAPTER 6

"For all my life I'll love you as you are"

I

If I say you look beautiful tonight
it's not because of the pencil on your eyes
or your perfume, or the cream you moisturise
your face with so it glistens in the light.
No— it's because no perfume can compare
to the scent of sleep nestling on your skin,
and there is no eyeliner that could win
over the faint circles of tiredness you bear
under your closing eyes. And why should you
use cream or powder when the dimming light
of the desk lamp beautifies the sight
of the least loved edges you'd hide from view?
If I say you look beautiful it's because I see
that in this moment you are beautiful to me.

II

I took a photograph of you today,
although I had no camera with me,
no flash but the beam of a sleepy day
that just awoke and stretched so I could see
your worn-out body wrapped safe in my sheet,
once the passion still showing on your breast
as a vermillion cloud, fumes of the heat
of our desire, has calmed. Your exposed chest
is heaving slowly, as though our lips sang
a lullaby to the small child in you;
thus peace embraced you, not even a bang
of the world's turmoil can wake you. I view
the delicate shape of your jaw, the lifeline
of my mouth's course, as you incline your head

towards me and I live to make it mine,
my lips alive on your skin till they're led
to yours, wet cherries on a summer night
of thirst, the moment a new life begins.
Your closed eyelids, moths flattering with delight,
as your hairs rustle like a violin's
chords, silence the most tuneful melody
of their orchestra on my pillowcase.
I'm glad I brought no camera with me,
for even though a lens can capture space,
it misses what the changing moments say —
but the mind listens before they depart.
So know this photograph of you will stay
alive and everpresent in my heart.

III

As I'm walking, careful not to destroy
the flowers that bloom afraid beneath my feet,
I can't help but think there would be more joy
in their life if they were gifted a seat
upon your hair. Even briefly, they'd live
in warmth and beauty, fondled by the beams
of your sunlight-like locks which would give
their moments meaning. If they stay here, dreams
of young buds away from the dust would perish
under a shoe or in the summer's drought.
They'll die either way but your curls would cherish
the bashful charms they hide. O what a thought—
such pure beauty with pure beauty combined!
you would nourish them with your light and they
would colour you with rainbow petals, kind
enough to endear you. But should I slay
them? Maybe they'll live and one day grow tall;
besides on your own you're the most beautiful of all.

IV

Where is your wing, my angel? did it break
when you were young and helpless, forced to fall
from heaven's innocence because a snake
got envious you could fly while it could crawl?
Where is your angel wing? Did someone tie
it once behind your back and grounded you
to earthly griefs, and made sure you won't fly
by binding a knot no one could undo?
Don't be afraid— I know you have a wing
you've been told not to use; for when my hand
is fondling your shoulder, I hear it sing
for help, to be caressed and once more stand.
And I will help you rise, relieve the pain,
and kiss your shoulders till wings grow again.

V

You say you want to stand under the spotlight
of a stage, take your guitar, and sing,
yet your first concert was on a summer night
when you performed and I heard, worshipping.
The light of a thousand stars was fixed on you
upon a stage of rocks and seaweeds, I could see
nothing else. Your voice was echoing through
the breeze like it was speakers, and the sea
applauded after the end of each song
with its excited waves. My tears were flames
of lighters being held up, swinging along
your melodies, ignited by the claims
your voice lays to my heart. Did it go well?
My love, the whole world fell under your spell.

VI

Your lips are like a rose covered in dew
in the morning; so wet and tender to touch!—
how could I ever keep my hands off you?
with each caress, the petals move with such
grace, as though brushed by the gentlest breeze
of sunrise. Rouge colour, more like strawberry
the further into the bloom my fingertips tease,
fiddling with the anthers. Thornless for me
alone, and so fragrant throughout the day,
the most beautiful scent that draws me near.
O, just one kiss and I will pull away!
But how can I? Amorous rose, smelling of sheer
humid wantonness, let me be the one
to breathe into you, and I'll be your sun.

VII

When I cup your cheek in my palm and trace
your delicate skin; when our foreheads cling
and my eyes silently admire your face,
I am seeking wrongs but I find nothing.
When my lips are with adoration pressed
to your jawline and shoulder; when I run
my fingers lower to fondle your breast,
I am searching for a fault but find none.
When scorched with yearning I go down to taste
your thighs and wet folds; when you come undone
and I cherish all the treasures below your waist
I'm looking for mistakes but find not one.
My kisses will endear your every scar,
for all my life I'll love you as you are.

VIII

I knew from the beginning that the hand
of beauty had touched it, but I could not
predict one day it would seduce my thought
into its sight forever. It was not planned
to fall in love with you, but when you gave
me that one smile, that treasure— it was done.
I loved you then so deeply, I forgave
all of my faults. I want to shout it is the sun,
the stars, and all my being, that single grin!
It coloured my mind and captured my heart,
but these are all abstractions— how to start
describing those small dimples on your skin
when I dare say I make you happy somehow?
Are they waves of an ocean, taking me
where the sky meets the water? Or maybe
they're just part of the wonder of you. I won't allow
anything to take it from me, or to exile
delight from it— for I live for this smile.

IX

Sweet love, there are times when you bow your head
and your long curly hair conceals the cheek
that's raining tears; a view much like a meek
weeping willow. With every teardrop shed
a little lake of sorrow starts to take
shape before you and helpless you stand there
while others bathe in it. O how unfair
to think that you are rooted to this ache,
seeing your reflection in it forever—
but dear heart, this is not who you can be!
you have been gifted with the harmony

of a swan whose graceful passings sever
the waters to make way for her. She sings
for lifetime devotion, queen of the pond
and of beauty, asking for no favours beyond
tranquillity, and by watching her kings
would learn how to be humble. A swan
once taught silence how to be beautiful— So
raise your head to see the real you, grow
wings out of weeping branches, and float on.

X

Your body is a temple and I, with head bowed
down to you, and lips worshiping your thighs,
your most faithful believer. Your arms the shroud
that clothes my resurrection, and your eyes
church candles that catch fire with every thought
I spend on you; what other way is there
but to adore when love becomes religion? Hot
the blessing of your breath each time, I swear,
I feel a miracle between your trembling legs,
and find within your smile all of my prayers
come true. And in my dreams your body begs
my fingers to be sacrificed in it in pairs,
sunk deeply into your depths until born
again. You need no scripture but your song,
my heartbeat's hymn, as my kisses adorn
your limbs, inside you revering as I belong.

XI

I've seen you angry and I've seen you sad,
I've listened to the music of your tears,
and gazed into your eyes that blaze with fears,

but still I don't think any of it bad.
I've seen you happy, I've seen you asleep,
adored the sunset colours on your face,
the clouds upon your eyelids, and I'll keep
admiring, for there's none I would erase.
I've seen you lustful and I've seen you sweet,
I've burned in the volcanoes of your heat
and melted in the honey of your kiss;
stay, for there's none I could afford to miss.
I've known sides of you, more than the above,
but I have found not one that I don't love.

CHAPTER 7

"You've made my mind, my heart a better place"

I

Can you thank the sun for giving out light
though she does not intend to? it's a mere
function of her existence, to be bright
for life without doing anything more to endear
her life-giving glow; for that so many admire
the shades of red she takes on through the day
and thank her for the mornings that do not expire;
thus I too often feel the blazing need to say
"thank you" for all that you have given me,
for the smiles that you gift but do not realise
they are like breath for me, and the beauty
of your song nourishing me like it's sunrise
and I midnight; how can I ever thank you
for reconciling the stars and the sun?
can I thank you for purely being you?
perhaps if I say: love, you are the one.

II

Love, every time you look at me, I feel
like I am all the stars in a night sky
without a moon; your loving eyes reveal
my feeble shine, once thought to be a firefly
wandering lost inside the darkness. Here,
inside your tender gaze, I am the universe,
a book whose mysteries are all made clear
at last, I am life's meaning turned to verse
and written on our city's walls; laid bare
like the aura of sunset till I see
none of this but myself. Inside your stare
I'm nothing more than me; I'm wholly me.

III

Each night I dream of a world where your name
is Inspiration; the vision is always the same.
As you walk, the footsteps you leave behind
are made of mixed up letters that combined
look like poems that I'll wake up to write.
There are ideas in your laughter, bright
and independent from the cold confines
of the world, for in its sound there are signs
of summer, a profound sense of liberty
that warms the heart. Your eyes are singing to me
and you call their melody Life. My dear,
can there be a song sweeter to the ear
that when I wake, I hear it still? It's true,
I was not asleep but awake to the real you,
your steps, your laughter and song, made to inspire
my dreams of poetry, my heart and my desire.

IV

One night, my love, I heard you sing for me
and I could swear your voice was summoning
the stars, turning your teary eyes into a sea
of the most tranquil water, reflecting
their fall and the scattered stardust. Your song
chased away all the clouds and the moon cried
for being on the half of the earth that was wrong,
too far to hear you. But I was there, beside
you, yet in a different world where time flows
with strokes of your fingers on the guitar,
with melodies that echo it is me you chose
to sing for. In that moment we were a star

ourselves, falling, a wish and its fulfilment,
and even as you sang, a whole new melody
was being created, the lyrics written as we went
on singing with silence, hearts whole and free.

v

You have an ear for
the magic of melodies
and you ask me
who would we be
without music?
You listen to it
like a child amazed
with magic tricks
and yet your heart
is a magician
practicing in secret
You have seen
how the tricks are made
but you still admire them
because you feel
they are not just craft
but the voice of the soul
Sometimes you perform
your magic for me
and when you ask
who would we be
without music
O, my love
how I long to answer
who would I be
without your music?

VI

There is a blazing fireplace in your eyes
and oft I seek its warmth for my hands, blue
and bruised from the cold, nearing to baptise
them in your cleansing fire. I look at you,
and see the sparks of the burning firewood
amidst the darkness that's surrounding me,
those dancing flames that show me all that's good
in life - had I known that your eyes would be
a fireplace in the dead of winter! Had
I known they would be consoling light
on the longest night soon! I'd be glad
to live in them forever - I'm all right
here in this comfort, warm without a doubt,
for I know this fireplace will not go out.

VII

O, how I loathe these pictures! go away,
bear your dull lifelessness out of my sight!
you think because you can make her smile stay
immortal, you could thus outshine the light
of its reality? you are wrong — how
could a lens ever capture those smooth waves
that gradually travel on her lips, a Now
in motion, followed by that voice that saves
my soul from void non-existence, which you
enhance with your stillness! surely you hold
her beauty like a dawn that morning can't undo,
you help me notice details on what's old
now, so that I can fall in love again
with who she was. But know that in her eyes

life gleams more vivid than sunlight, no pen
or lens can keep; that is when by surprise
I see the living charm you can't convey,
and fall in love with who she is each day.

VIII

In a sky of a million stars ours is
the one which will not fall to the abyss
no matter how many years pass. If we
ever feel like we're sinking in a sea
of people, remember love taught us how to
breathe underwater. Since I am with you,
I've never looked up to the sky and thought
it is not beautiful— one night I even caught
the stars for the first time smiling at me.
Those feeble lights upon the Christmas tree
have not burned out, nor am I in a haste
to dream— the sunsets now don't go to waste.
Stay— our tears are nothing more than a knife
that can't cut. I don't want to spend a life
scribbling poetry about how I lost you,
knowing we loved but didn't make it through.
In you at last I found a certainty,
so please, do not take it away from me.

IX

There is a war in me I cannot end
and though I win most battles
I have lost so many heartbeats
that could have lived another day

to make love to you again.
I have sacrificed so many smiles
and come back to you with
a thousand open wounds
you cared enough to stitch.
My ears will not stop bleeding
from the rattling sound of guns,
my thoughts, which without mercy
shoot me down over and over.
Then— you walk without fear
in the battlefield but bullets
always seem to miss you.
You give me your hand
and steady me on my unstable legs.
Perhaps at night we should
sneak into the enemy's camp
and steal their weapons.

X

The spring air soothes me as I lay my head
upon your lap once more. I feel as though
the world is an ocean whose currents spread
further than I can conceive, and I go
along, a reckless traveller floating on
the ship you've created with your embrace.
Strong and stable in the storm, not a pawn
of the winds but master of them, you pace
on the waves firm, without fear to go down,
always making sure that I will not drown.

XI

There are times when we talk about our hair
like they are politicians, and our hips
memoirs excavated from the dirt. "Bare
the words engraved on your body, your lips
are the gods of today", they say to me.
And so I thought that I may as well speak
of my fringe, seemingly combed by conformity
as it falls in perfect fashion upon my cheek.
We no more fight with shields, so I had to
protect myself from the Big Brother eyes
of the world. I was afraid— I am. But you
came close to me and lifted the disguise
of this cool fringe, and saw that my eyebrow
should have been plucked at least two days ago,
that fear makes me sweat, that I bear a frown
which should stay caged, or else my sorrows show.
You pressed your lips to my forehead, to skin
oily so what it touches slips away,
yet your kiss lingers still— I let you in,
behind the fringe that's slowly turning grey.
If you are wandering what I am on
about— well, in simple words, you've touched me
so deeply in the heart, I can't breathe if you're gone,
and that's how they say it in the 21st century.

XII

You make me so happy that I can fight
the whole world if I must. How could you fear
that I would leave, when it's for you I write,
for you I breathe? How could love disappear

when it is in my veins, refreshed anew
day after day that I live in your gaze,
and my heart jumps at the mere thought of you?
You said you do not like the word always
and all my life I doubted everything
until now that I found a single certainty:
our love. Could I live without hearing you sing
the essence of your true self? I stay for me,
for you, but mostly for us. Because I see
no other way; because, my love, we cannot be
anything else in life but together.

XIII

Listening to the sweet sound of your song
in peace, and still strong enough to lie
cradled up in your arms where I belong,
old and loved— this is how I want to die.
But standing like conquerors at the peak
of a mountain, half asleep on a plane
with our fingers intertwined, cheek to cheek
making love at midday— under the rain
with jeans splashed from a bus, the fullmoon's glow
our only dress as we lay by the sea—
slipping on the ice, dancing through the snow,
always restless and passionate and free—
on our bed eating noodles every day,
embraced, with those caresses that forgive
all of our faults and force our fears away—
with you, love— this is how I want to live.

XIV

You are sunlight sneaking through branches of
the forest that's been growing in my mind
for years. But now with you, my sun, my love,
the once dark trees around me are designed
with different colours, sometimes they appear
almost beautiful to me. Now listening to
the rustling of the leaves does not inspire fear
within my heart. Their song is calling to
you, singing hymns in the hope you will feed
them with your light. Now I can see the way
being laid ahead of me, I do not bleed
tripping over roots in the darkness. Stay
and the memory of shadows will fade completely
from my thoughts. Now together we will chase
the night and maybe I will also help you see
you've made my mind, my heart a better place.

XV

Sometimes when I lay my head on your breast
I realise how glad I truly feel
that looking from the window we can steal
a glimpse of the blue sky and drive the stress
of our routine away— How glad I am for
the stains on the walls, reminding us of
the wine we spilt one night when drunk on love
we failed to control the hands shaking to adore
each other's skin— How glad I am for these
dead hairs tangled between our sheets, for they
must have fallen once when I ached to squeeze
your locks while being inside you. I dare say

I'm glad Sundays have many hours, for bliss,
adventure, or just sitting down to hear
your laugh— But most of all I'm glad for this;
I get to feel such love and you are here.

XVI

Dear, if a star had fallen for every
wish of mine that came true because of you,
none would be left, the sky would be empty,
and stars would be flying like fireflies through
the cities, sitting on the trees at night.
And if I were asking a daisy every day
about the truth of your love, plucking away
her petals, the world by now would be quite
short on oxygen and petals would fly
against the wind like swarms of birds. Dear,
can you see that you're making the sky cry
meteor showers by making my dreams cohere
with my reality? There aren't enough flowers to
assure me your love is real like your eyes
do with a look. Under these starry skies,
among the blooms, I am happy because of you.

About the Author

Lina Katsorchi was born in Athens, where she still lives today. She holds an MA in English Literature, Culture, and Theory from the University of Sussex, UK, after completing her BA in English Language and Literature at the National and Kapodistrian University of Athens. In her free time she loves to practice martial arts and scribble poetry. Her poetry collection Constellation is an attempt to give voice to the heart.

www.ingramcontent.com/pod-product-compliance
Lightning Source LLC
Chambersburg PA
CBHW071757080526
44588CB00013B/2273
* 9 7 8 1 9 1 2 3 1 5 8 1 9 *